Writing with Prayer

Second Edition

Michael McHugh

Christian Liberty Academy
Handwriting Program

Written by Michael J. McHugh
Copy editing by Christopher Kou
Cover design by Robert Fine
Illustrations by Ron Farris
Layout and graphics by Christopher and Timothy Kou at
imagineering studios, inc.

A publication of
Christian Liberty Press
502 West Euclid Avenue
Arlington Heights, IL 60004
www.christianlibertypress.com

ISBN 978-1-930367-87-6
           1-930367-87-2

Text set in Berkeley
Handwriting set in Zaner-Bloser except for "Q" and "k," and ","

Printed in the United States of America

Contents

Preface

This is the third text in the Christian Liberty Academy series in handwriting. We remind you that one key to teaching success is reducing frustration in both parent and student. A wise teacher will not fail to take into account the maturity of the children so they can enjoy their handwriting activities without constant boredom or extreme fatigue. Learning need not be a tedious exercise. The staff at Christian Liberty Academy has taken care to design each lesson to fit the attention span of the average primary student. Patience, prayer, and persistence are indispensable for success in teaching primary handwriting.

It is very important for instructors to realize that extra drill work (on the blackboard and practice paper) must be assigned for each and every concept in the textbook. In addition, have the students practice each exercise before writing their work in the book. In the first and second grade, the student's careful attention to the component strokes of letters becomes important. Special attention must also be spent on the development of good oral and visual memory of alphabetical order. Alphabet flash cards, games, and songs are convenient ways to establish this critical skill.

This text will review manuscript handwriting briefly. If extensive review is needed, we recommend placement in one of our previous texts. Transition from manuscript to cursive is completed by the end of the second semester.

Both gross and fine motor skills are involved in handwriting. Certain abilities are generally found at this beginning level of development:

1.   Good control of pencils, scissors, buttons, and zippers.
2.   Ability to follow a series of spoken or written directions.
3.   Ability to trace lines.
4.   Ability to draw figures such as circles and squares.
5.   Ability to distinguish between proper and improper spacing.

This text contains activities to develop and maintain the above skills.

Good handwriting is an essential skill of expression and communication. Time spent on handwriting is well spent. May the God of all grace help you develop students who will desire to write legibly and attractively for the glory of God.

In Christian fellowship,
Michael J. McHugh

Introduction to Parents

After working with manuscript for a year or so, most students quite naturally start to introduce cursive into their writing. The odd cursive letter or word may already be appearing in your students' work. This natural ambition to grow up is better directed and channeled than discouraged.

Manuscript should continue to be practiced, however, to improve mastery. Even as adults we still have many occasions when manuscript is required: filling out forms and job applications, for example. Allow the students to make the transition at their own pace, but use this text to provide guidance as soon as cursive starts to appear in their work.

Look for these signs of readiness to begin cursive:

1. Good performance on this text's manuscript review.

2. The student's taking initiative in trying to reproduce cursive independently.

3. The ability to write three sentences in manuscript without tiring or losing control of good form.

Provide opportunities for your students to read cursive as well as write it. For a while, students will probably have more confidence in their manuscript work–it is more familiar. After two or three months' work with cursive, most students will come to prefer cursive as "easier," "faster," and "more grown up."

The readiness activities that follow are a brief review of manuscript letters, a brief introduction to style (capitalization and punctuation), and practice with some important cursive strokes. As when writing manuscript, students should:

1. Sit up straight, leaning forward slightly.

2. Rest both arms on the desk.

3. Keep both feet on the floor.

4. Relax.

Handwriting will improve if practiced every day. Fifteen to twenty minutes a day is sufficient at this grade level. If the student is improving at a slower pace than is reasonable, chances are that the student needs more time doing readiness activities first. Don't be tempted to increase handwriting practice time–when readiness skills are developed enough, the student will improve in handwriting skills most efficiently without being pushed.

Left-Handedness

Make sure your students are using the hand that is most natural for them. Remember that left-handed students will have a more difficult task, because the movement from left to right across the page is awkward for the left hand.

Proper Writing Posture

Some children write with their left hand. This picture shows how they should sit when they write.

Some children write with their right hand. This picture shows how they should sit when they write.

Some children write with their left hand. This picture shows how they should hold their pencil.

Some children write with their right hand. This picture shows how they should hold their pencil.

Some children write with their left hand. This picture shows how they should stand at the chalkboard.

Some children write with their right hand. This picture shows how they should stand at the chalkboard.

Lowercase Cursive Alphabet

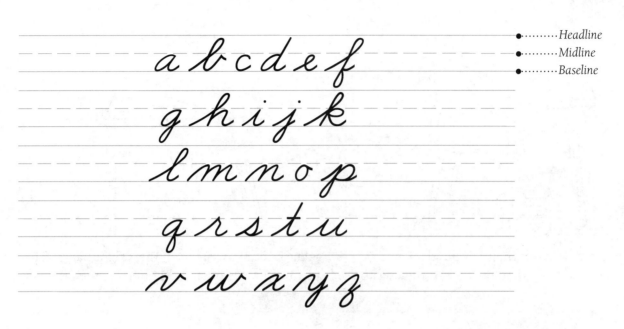

Headline
Midline
Baseline

Uppercase Cursive Alphabet

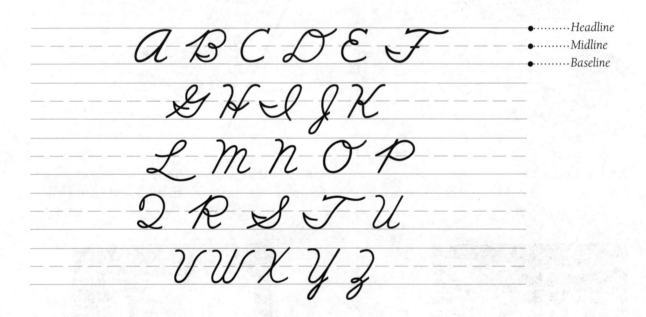

Headline
Midline
Baseline

4

Manuscript Review Aa-Ii

Practice writing upper and lower case letters. Trace each letter and write five more on each line.

Aa

Bb

Cc

Dd

Ee

Ff

Gg

Hh

Ii

In the space below, practice writing any letters that are hard for you to form.

If students have difficulty forming any letters, they should practice writing them on a separate sheet of paper or on a chalkboard.

Practice writing upper and lower case letters. Trace each letter and write five more on each line.

Jj

Kk

Ll

Mm

Nn

Oo

Pp

Qq

Rr

In the space below, practice writing any letters that are hard for you to form.

If students have difficulty forming any letters, they should practice writing them on a separate sheet of paper or on a chalkboard.

Manuscript Review Ss-Zz

Practice writing upper and lower case letters. Trace each letter and write five more on each line.

Ss

Tt

Uu

Vv

Ww

Xx

Yy

Zz

In the space below, practice writing any letters that are hard for you to form.

If students have difficulty forming any letters, they should practice writing them on a separate sheet of paper or on a chalkboard.

Punctuation: Period, Question Mark, and Exclamation Point

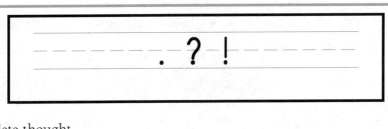

A **period** ends a complete thought.
Doesn't a **question mark** follow a question?
An **exclamation point** follows a sentence containing a strong idea!

Trace the example sentences below. Watch your punctuation!

We must love one another.

Who is on the Lord's side?

The walls of Jericho fell flat!

Trace each sentence and put the correct punctuation mark at the end of the sentences below.

When will you trust God

Jesus is risen from the dead

The Bible is the Word of God

Capitalization

Choose the correct word from the list below and write it at the beginning of the line to complete each sentence. Remember to use a capital letter at the beginning of each sentence. All words that refer to the name of God must also be capitalized.

Bibles	Church	America
Pray	Love	Fathers

_____ contain the Old and New Testaments.

_____ leaders are called ministers.

_____ is a beautiful country.

_____ to the Lord each day.

_____ must rule their households well.

_____ the Lord at all times.

Rewrite each word in the space provided below, replacing the first letter of each word with a capital letter.

united states   president   pastor   god

_____

_____

Writing Sentences

Trace the first example sentence. Copy each of the additional sentences in the space provided. Be sure to leave the proper spacing between each word.

The Lord is my shepherd.

Remember the Sabbath day.

All glory belongs to Almighty God.

Jesus Christ is King of Kings.

Jezebel was a wicked woman.

Ahab stole the vineyard of Naboth.

The Lord is my Shepherd.

Writing Sentences

Trace the first example sentence. Copy each of the additional sentences in the space provided. Be sure to leave the proper spacing between each word.

My hope is in the Lord.

David was the king of Israel.

Elisha was a faithful prophet of Jehovah.

We must not break the Law of God.

The Creator made animals and all things.

Be quick to guard your heart.

The Bible contains sixty-six books.

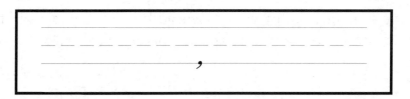

The comma is used for several different purposes. One use of the comma is to separate the day and year when writing a date. A comma is not needed when a specific day is not included.

Example: September 11, 2001

Copy the dates listed below in the space provided. Place a comma between the day and the year.

March 4 1957   April 14 2000

July 10 1921   June 1 1941

May 4 2003   August 27 1930

More Punctuation: The Comma

A comma should also be used to separate a city from a state.

Example: Chicago, Illinois

Copy the following sentences. Place a comma between the city and state.

Our family drove to Miami Florida.

My friend Tim lives in Dallas Texas.

My mother was born in Denver Colorado.

A comma should also be used to separate a listing of more than two items on a list.

Example: The doctor had a needle, knife, and bandage.

Copy the following sentences. Place a comma after each word on the list.

The cook used eggs bread and bacon.

Connel Michael and Eric went camping.

Writing Sentences with Punctuation

Copy each of the sentences listed below. Be sure to add the proper punctuation marks and capital letters.

Example:

Does Mark like to read?

Does Mark like to read?

Andy, Kim, and Ron play checkers.

The United States began on July 4, 1776.

My father works in Lansing, Michigan.

Did Andrew read his Bible last night?

Jesus Christ is the Son of God.

Christmas is a celebration of Christ's birth.

Writing Sentences with Punctuation

Copy each of the sentences listed below. Be sure to add proper puctuation and capital letters.

Do not touch the fire!

Happy is he who keeps the Law of God.

The rose was red, yellow, and orange.

The love of God is pure and free.

Who took my bag of candy?

Whitman was born on July 1, 1959.

Jesus is the Way, the Truth, and the Life.

Writing a Paragraph in Manuscript

A paragraph contains a particular idea that is separate from other ideas put forth by the writer. Most paragraphs contain more than one sentence, but only one main thought or idea.

Copy the paragraph below in the space provided on the next page. The model paragraph is from Matthew 22: 37-40

Jesus said unto him, Thou shalt love the Lord thy God with all thy heart, and with all thy soul, and with all thy mind. This is the first and great commandment. And the second is like unto it, Thou shalt love thy neighbor as thyself. On these two commandments hang all the law and the prophets.

Writing a Paragraph in Manuscript

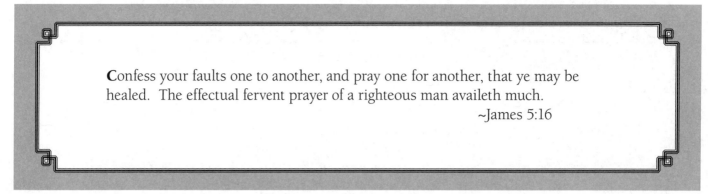

Confess your faults one to another, and pray one for another, that ye may be healed. The effectual fervent prayer of a righteous man availeth much.

~James 5:16

Instructor Tips

Make sure your students slowly stretch out their hand and arms before beginning to write. Encourage them to relax as they practice.

Chapter Check-up

How well can you write?
Do your best work as you copy these sentences:
The Lord is my Shepherd. My hope is in Jesus Christ.

Answer the following questions.   Circle

1. Am I keeping all letters on the baseline?   Yes   No
2. Am I shaping every letter correctly?   Yes   No
3. Am I making each letter the correct height?   Yes   No
4. Am I spacing letters evenly?   Yes   No
5. Am I leaving space between words?   Yes   No
6. Am I leaving extra space between sentences?   Yes   No
7. Am I including punctuation?   Yes   No
8. Am I remembering to capitalize?   Yes   No

Letters I write well:

Letters I need to practice:

Cursive Readiness: Basic Strokes

Trace the right-to-left slanted strokes. Make ten strokes on each line.

Trace the left-to-right slanted strokes. Make ten strokes on each line.

Trace the circles counter-clockwise. Make ten circles on each line.

Trace the circles clockwise. Make ten circles on each line.

Trace the undercurves. Make ten curves on each line.

Starting Strokes, Connecting Strokes, and Loops

Trace the starting strokes. Make ten strokes on each line.

Trace the horizontal loops. Make ten loops on each line.

Trace the starting strokes. Make ten strokes on each line.

Trace the forward loops. Make ten loops on each line.

Trace the underloops. Make ten underloops on each line.

Basic Curves

Trace the double undercurves. Make ten undercurves on each line.

Trace the forward curves. Make ten curves on each line.

Trace the double overcurves. Make ten overcurves on each line.

Trace the triple overcurves. Make ten overcurves on each line.

21

c o a

Instructions

1. Start slightly below the midline, then curve back and down to the baseline.
2. Continue the curve up to the beginning and pause.
3. Slant down to the baseline and finish with an undercurve half way.

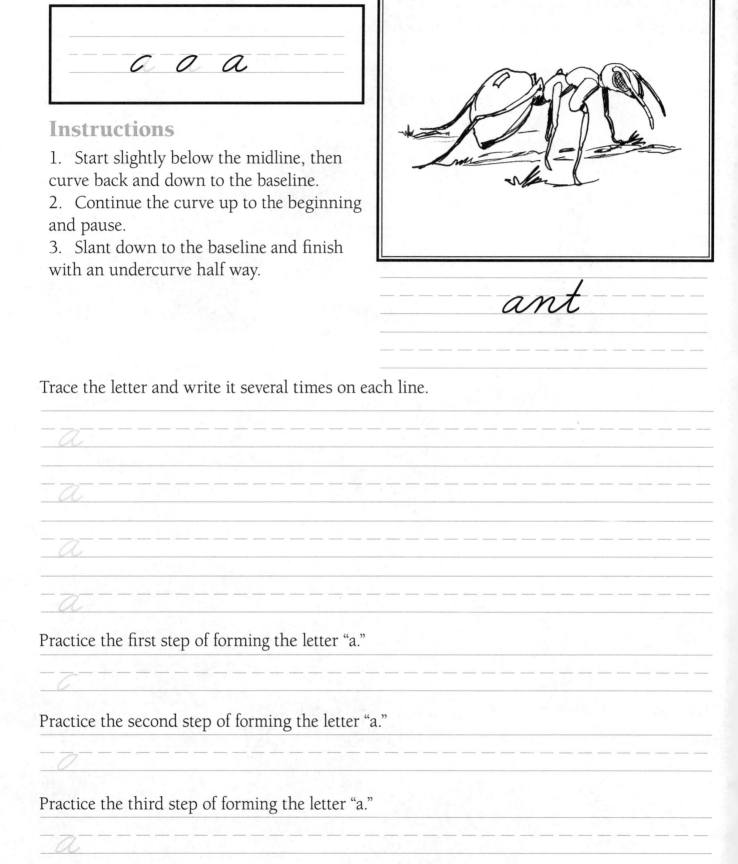

ant

Trace the letter and write it several times on each line.

a

a

a

a

Practice the first step of forming the letter "a."

c

Practice the second step of forming the letter "a."

o

Practice the third step of forming the letter "a."

a

Provide extra practice as needed on separate lined paper.

Instructions

1. Start with a forward loop.
2. Curve up towards the midline.
3. Finish with a small hook to the right.

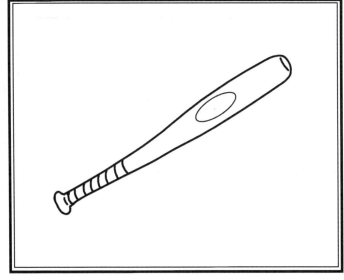

bat

Trace the letter and write it several times on each line.

Write the word " baa."

Write the word "abba."

Provide extra practice as needed on separate lined paper.

C   C

Instructions

1. Start at the midline and curve back and down to the baseline.
2. Finish with an undercurve.

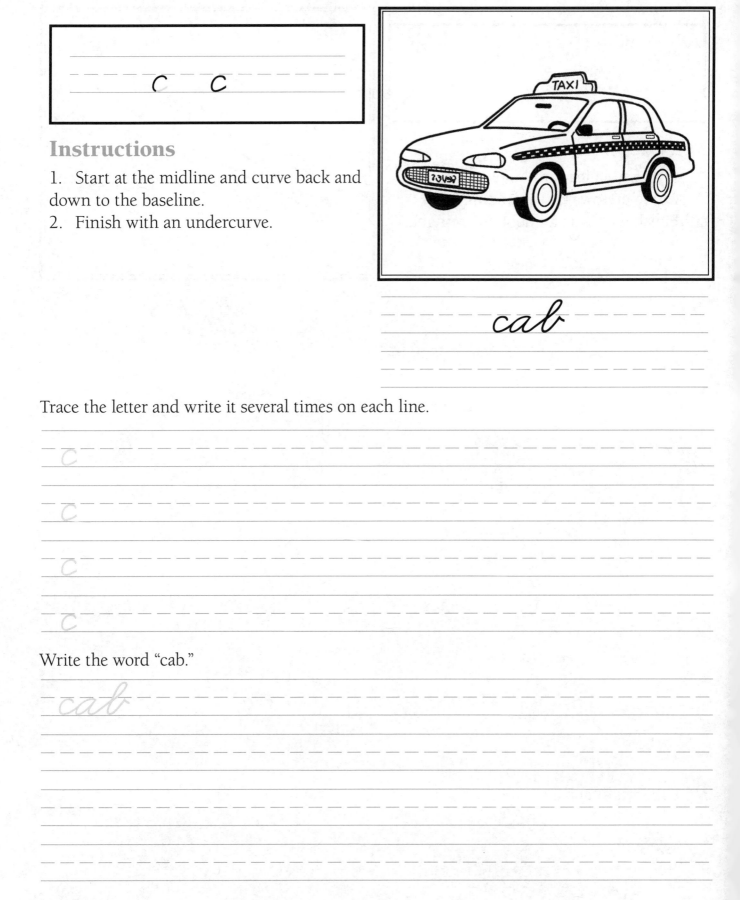

cab

Trace the letter and write it several times on each line.

C

C

C

C

Write the word "cab."

cab

Provide extra practice as needed on separate lined paper.

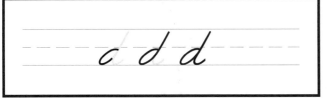

Instructions

1. Start with a forward curve.
2. Continue up towards the headline.
3. Retrace the line downwards to the baseline and finish with a small hook to the right.

dad

Trace the letter and write it several times on each line.

d

d

d

d

Write the word "bad."

bad

Write the word "add."

add

Provide extra practice as needed on separate lined paper.

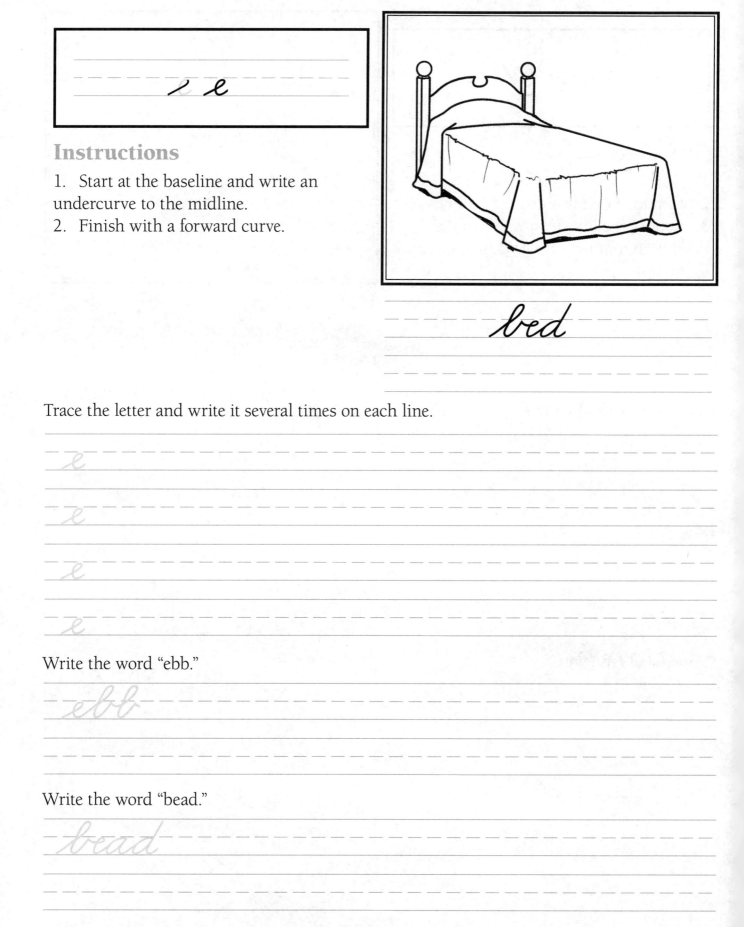

Instructions

1. Start at the baseline and write an undercurve to the midline.
2. Finish with a forward curve.

bed

Trace the letter and write it several times on each line.

e

e

e

e

Write the word "ebb."

ebb

Write the word "bead."

bead

Provide extra practice as needed on separate lined paper.

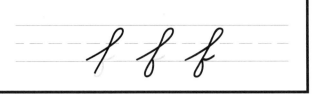

Instructions

1. Start with a forward loop and continue down past the baseline.
2. Curve back up to where the baseline and your line cross.
3. Finish with a small hook to the right.

fan

Trace the letter and write it several times on each line.

f

f

f

f

Write the word "face."

face

Write the word "deaf."

deaf

Provide extra practice as needed on separate lined paper.

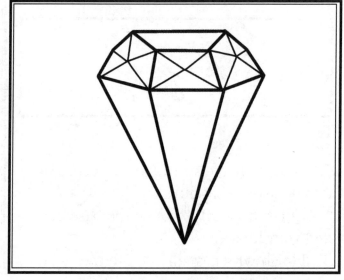

Instructions

1. Start with a forward curve.
2. Continue up to the midline where you began.
3. Curve down below the baseline.
4. Loop back up above the baseline crossing your last stroke at the baseline.

gem

Trace the letter and write it several times on each line.

g

g

g

g

Write the word "gaff."

gaff

Write the word "gag."

gag

Provide extra practice as needed on separate lined paper.

Instructions

1. Start with a forward loop.
2. Write an overcurve.
3. Finish with a small hook to the right.

head

Trace the letter and write it several times on each line.

h

h

h

h

Write the word "he."

he

Write the word "had."

had

Provide extra practice as needed on separate lined paper.

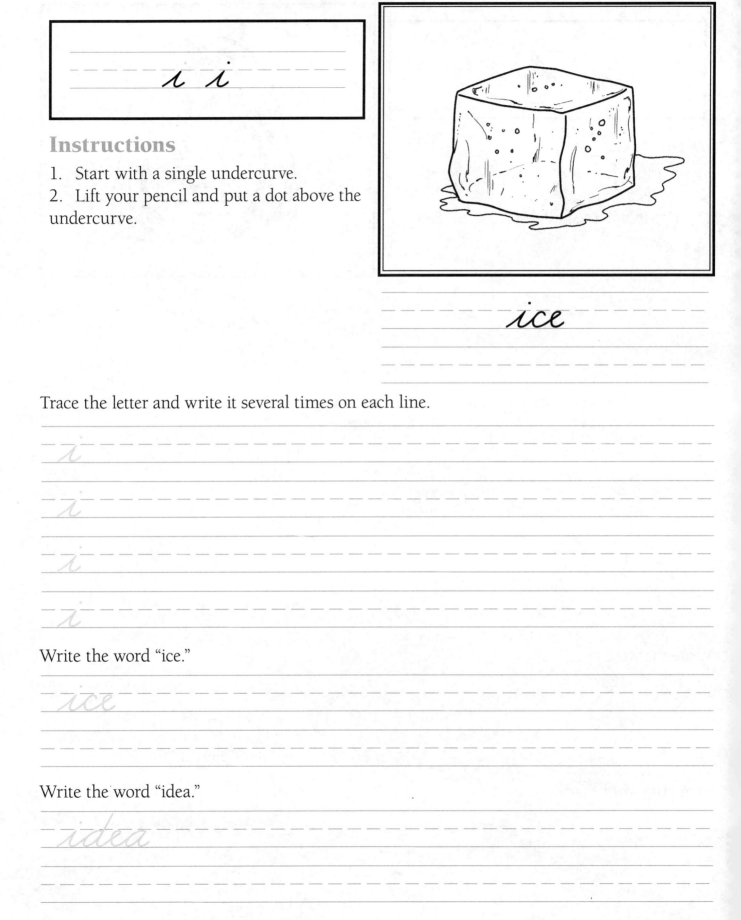

_i i_

Instructions

1. Start with a single undercurve.
2. Lift your pencil and put a dot above the undercurve.

ice

Trace the letter and write it several times on each line.

_i_

_i_

_i_

_i_

Write the word "ice."

ice

Write the word "idea."

idea

Provide extra practice as needed on separate lined paper.

Instructions

1. Start at the baseline and write an undercurve to the midline.
2. Curve down below the baseline.
3. Loop back up to the midline crossing your last stroke at the baseline.
4. Lift your pencil and put a dot above the first stroke.

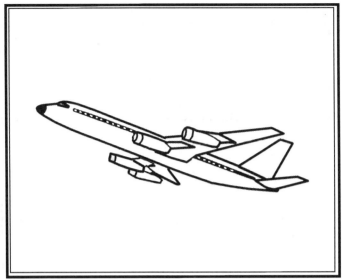

jet

Trace the letter and write it several times on each line.

j

j

j

j

Write the word "jab."

jab

Write the word "jig."

jig

Provide extra practice as needed on separate lined paper.

Instructions

1. Start with a forward loop.
2. Without lifting your pencil make a horizontal loop under the midline.
3. Finish with an undercurve.

kick

Trace the letter and write it several times on each line.

k

k

k

k

Write the word "kid."

kid

Write the word "keg."

keg

Provide extra practice as needed on separate lined paper.

Instructions

1. Start with a forward loop.
2. Finish with an undercurve.

leaf

Trace the letter and write it several times on each line.

l

l

l

l

Write the word "label."

label

Write the word "lead."

lead

Provide extra practice as needed on separate lined paper.

Instructions

1. Start at the baseline and curve up to the midline. Go back down to make an overcurve.
2. Make three overcurves without lifting your pencil.
3. Finish with an undercurve.

man

Trace the letter and write it several times on each line.

m

m

m

m

Write the word "mad."

mad

Write the word "maid."

maid

Provide extra practice as needed on separate lined paper.

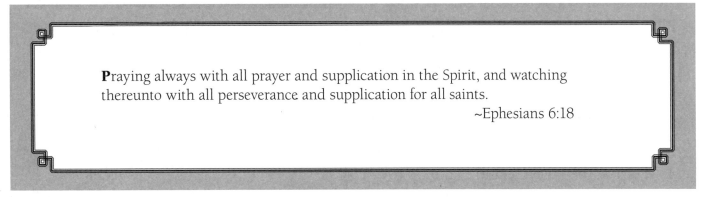

> **P**raying always with all prayer and supplication in the Spirit, and watching thereunto with all perseverance and supplication for all saints.
>
> ~Ephesians 6:18

Instructor Tips

Encourage the students to evaluate their own handwriting. Acknowledge their progress. Respect differences in style while correcting poor form.

Chapter Check-up

Are you ready to write? Do your best work as you copy these phrases.

the big bed   **he did like ice**

Answer the following questions.   Circle

1. Do all my letters slant in the same direction?   Yes   No
2. Am I shaping every letter correctly?   Yes   No
3. Are all the letters in one word connected?   Yes   No
4. Am I spacing letters evenly?   Yes   No

Letters I write well:

Letters I need to practice:

Instructions

1. Start at the baseline and curve up to the midline. Go back down to make an overcurve.
2. Make two overcurves without lifting your pencil.
3. Finish with an undercurve.

nail

Trace the letter and write it several times on each line.

n

n

n

n

Write the word "name."

name

Write the word "nice."

nice

Provide extra practice as needed on separate lined paper.

o o

Instructions

1. Start by making a circle between the baseline and the midline.
2. Finish with a small hook to the right.

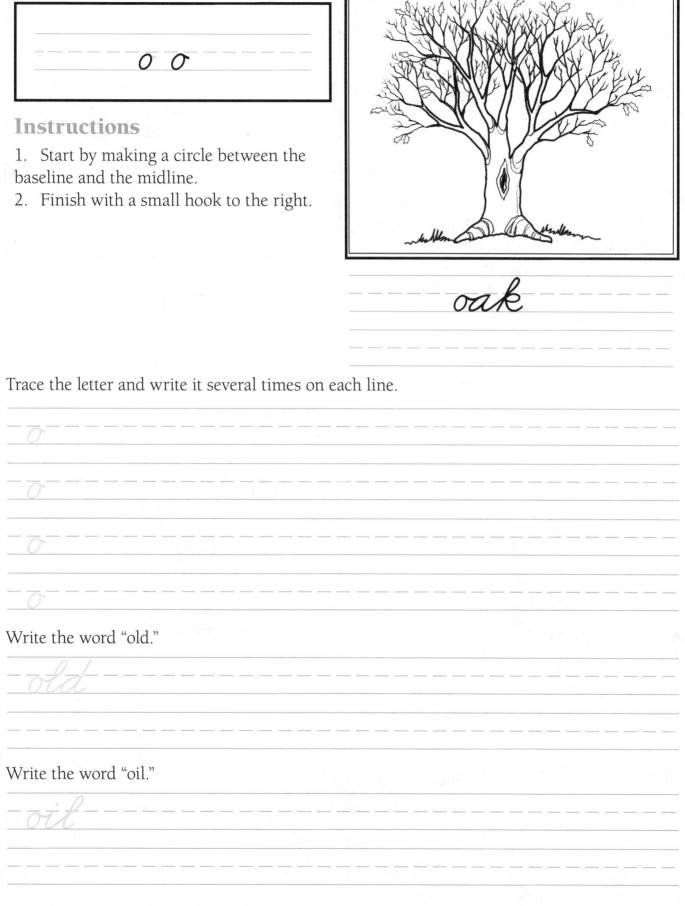

oak

Trace the letter and write it several times on each line.

o

o

o

o

Write the word "old."

old

Write the word "oil."

oil

Provide extra practice as needed on separate lined paper.

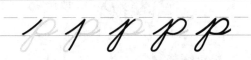

Instructions

1. Start at the baseline and write an undercurve to the midline.
2. Curve down below the baseline.
3. Loop back up to the midline crossing your last stroke at the baseline.
4. Continue to curve down and back to where your last line crosses the baseline without lifting your pencil.
5. Finish with an undercurve.

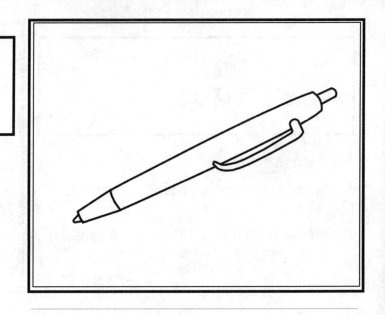

pen

Trace the letter and write it several times on each line.

p

p

p

p

Write the word "pin."

pin

Write the word "pond."

pond

Provide extra practice as needed on separate lined paper.

q q q q

Instructions

1. Start with a forward curve.
2. Continue up to the midline and go back down past the baseline.
3. Curve up to where your last stroke crosses the baseline.
4. Finish with an undercurve.

quail

Trace the letter and write it several times on each line.

q

q

q

q

Write the word "queen."

queen

Write the word "quail."

quail

Provide extra practice as needed on separate lined paper.

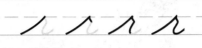

Instructions

1. Start with an undercurve.
2. Without lifting your pencil make a small hook to the right.
3. Curve down to the baseline.
4. Finish with an undercurve.

raccoon

Trace the letter and write it several times on each line.

r

r

r

r

Write the word "rice."

rice

Write the word "real."

real

Provide extra practice as needed on separate lined paper.

40

Instructions

1. Start with an undercurve.
2. Curve back down to the baseline and then back to your last stroke.
3. Finish with an undercurve.

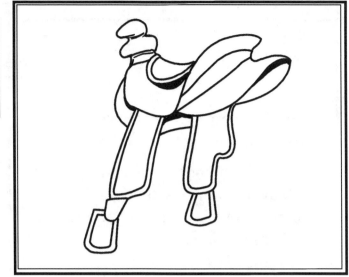

saddle

Trace the letter and write it several times on each line.

s

s

s

s

Write the word "sail."

sail

Write the word "sacred."

sacred

Provide extra practice as needed on separate lined paper.

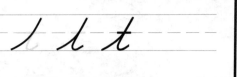

Instructions

1. Start with an undercurve and continue all the way up to the headline.
2. Go back down to the baseline and make an undercurve.
3. Cross the "t" at the midline.

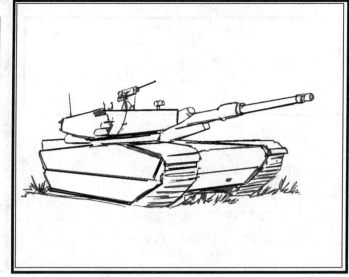

tank

Trace the letter and write it several times on each line.

t

t

t

t

Write the word "kitten."

kitten

Write the word "tape."

tape

Provide extra practice as needed on separate lined paper.

Instructions

1. Start at the baseline with an undercurve.
2. Make two more undercurves without lifting your pencil.

umpire

Trace the letter and write it several times on each line.

u

u

u

u

Write the word "under."

under

Write the word "umbrella."

umbrella

Provide extra practice as needed on separate lined paper.

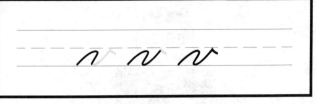

Instructions

1. Start with an overcurve.
2. Curve back up to the midline.
3. Finish with a small hook to the right.

vase

Trace the letter and write it several times on each line.

v

v

v

v

Write the word "vail."

vail

Write the word "vacuum."

vacuum

Provide extra practice as needed on separate lined paper.

44

Instructions

1. Start at the baseline with an undercurve.
2. Make two more undercurves without lifting you pencil.
3. Finish with a small hook to the right.

wagon

Trace the letter and write it several times on each line.

w

w

w

w

Write the word "wag."

wag

Write the word "war."

war

Provide extra practice as needed on separate lined paper.

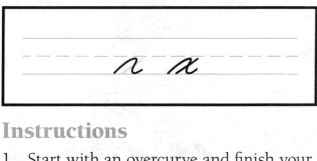

Instructions

1. Start with an overcurve and finish your stroke with an undercurve.

2. Lift your pencil and cross the "x" from the midline to the baseline.

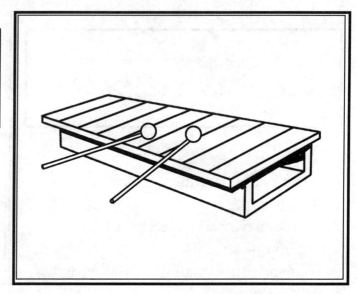

xylophone

Trace the letter and write it several times on each line.

x

x

x

x

Write the word "oxen."

oxen

Write the word "xerox."

xerox

Provide extra practice as needed on separate lined paper.

46

y y y y

Instructions

1. Start with an overcurve.
2. Continue into an undercurve.
3. Curve back down below the baseline.
4. Loop back up above the baseline.

yarn

Trace the letter and write it several times on each line.

y

y

y

y

Write the word "yogurt."

yogurt

Write the word "yard."

yard

Provide extra practice as needed on separate lined paper.

Instructions

1. Start with an overcurve.
2. Curve down below the baseline.
3. Loop back up above the baseline crossing your last stroke at the baseline.

zebra

Trace the letter and write it several times on each line.

z

z

z

z

Write the word "zinc."

zinc

Write the word "zoo."

zoo

Provide extra practice as needed on separate lined paper.

48

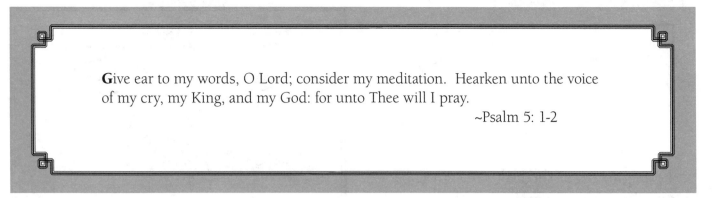

Give ear to my words, O Lord; consider my meditation. Hearken unto the voice of my cry, my King, and my God: for unto Thee will I pray.

~Psalm 5: 1-2

Instructor Tips

Encourage your students to see how many ways there are to use their handwriting skills every day. Remind your students not to rush through their work, for haste makes waste.

Chapter Check-up

Are you ready to write? Do your best work as you write out the following sentence.
The quick brown fox jumps over the lazy dog.

Answer the following questions.   Circle

1.	Do all my letters slant in the same direction?	Yes	No
2.	Am I shaping every letter correctly?	Yes	No
3.	Are all the letters in one word connected?	Yes	No
4.	Am I spacing letters evenly?	Yes	No

Letters I write well:

Letters I need to practice:

Instructions

1. Beginning at the headline, curve back and down to the baseline.
2. Undercurve back to the headline and pause.
3. Retrace and slant to the baseline.
4. Finish with an undercurve.

Angel

Trace the letter and write it several times on each line.

a

a

a

a

Write the word "Arctic"

Arctic

Write the sentence "An alligator can swim fast." Remember to use a period.

Provide extra practice as needed on separate lined paper.

Instructions

1. Start slightly below the midline with an undercurve.
2. Slant back and down to the baseline.
3. Continue at the top by forming a forward loop to the midline.
4. Complete the bottom loop so it touches the vertical stroke.
5. Finish with an undercurve half way to the midline.

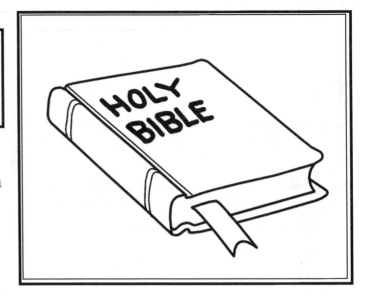

Bible

Trace the letter and write it several times on each line.

Write the word "Bethlehem"

Bethlehem

Write the sentence "Before breakfast you should read your Bible."

Provide extra practice as needed on separate lined paper.

51

C C

Crown

Instructions

1. Start at the headline with a small notch at the top and curve down to the baseline.
2. Finish with an undercurve.

Trace the letter and write it several times on each line.

C

C

C

C

Write the word "Christ."

Christ

Write the sentence "Charity never fails."

Provide extra practice as needed on separate lined paper.

Instructions

1. Start close to the headline and curve down to the baseline.
2. Loop up and curve back down to the baseline.
3. Curve back up to the headline and to your first stroke.
4. Finish with a loop downwards and curve back up to the headline.

David

Trace the letter and write it several times on each line.

Write the word "Dad."

Write the sentence "David loved to pray and sing."

Provide extra practice as needed on separate lined paper.

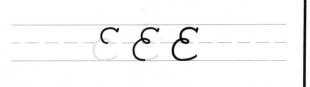

Instructions

1. Start at the headline with a small notch and curve down to the midline.
2. Loop up and curve down to the baseline.
3. Finish with an undercurve.

Esther

Trace the letter and write it several times on each line.

E

E

E

E

Write the word "Eskimo."

Eskimo

Write the sentence "Eskimos live in igloos."

Provide extra practice as needed on separate lined paper.

Instructions

1. Start a little under the headline and curve down to the baseline.
2. Continue to curve up back to the midline and hook to the right.
3. Lift your pencil and, at the headline, make a notch and cross the "F" by making a horizontal double curve.
4. Cross the "F" again at the midline.

Family

Trace the letter and write it several times on each line.

Write the word "Faith."

Faith

Write the sentence "Faith is the victory through Christ."

Provide extra practice as needed on separate lined paper.

G G G G

Instructions

1. Start at the baseline and curve up past the midline.
2. Loop back down to the midline and curve up to halfway between the midline and headline.
3. Curve down to the baseline.
4. Finish by curving back up to the midline and hooking back to the right.

Giraffe

Trace the letter and write it several times on each line.

G

G

G

G

Write the word "Grace."

Grace

Write the sentence "God alone gives saving grace."

Provide extra practice as needed on separate lined paper.

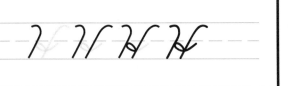

Instructions

1. Start by curving at the headline down to the baseline.
2. Lift your pencil and start another line on the right by curving the other way down to the baseline.
3. Continue and make a horizontal loop below the midline.
4. Finish by making a hook to the midline.

Harp

Trace the letter and write it several times on each line.

Write the word "Holy."

Write the sentence "God makes us holy and happy."

Provide extra practice as needed on separate lined paper.

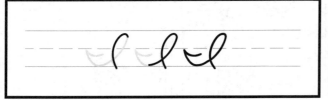

Instructions

1. Start a bit below the baseline and curve up to the headline.
2. Loop back and down to the baseline.
3. Finish by curving back up to the midline and hooking back to the right.

Israel

Trace the letter and write it several times on each line.

el

el

el

el

Write the word "Irish."

Irish

Write the sentence "It is God who rules over us."

Provide extra practice as needed on separate lined paper.

58

Instructions

1. Start a bit below the baseline and curve up to the headline.
2. Loop back down to below the baseline crossing your first stroke at the baseline.
3. Loop back up above the baseline crossing both of your strokes at the baseline.

John

Trace the letter and write it several times on each line.

Write the word "Jesus."

Write the sentence "Jesus Christ is God."

Provide extra practice as needed on separate lined paper.

Instructions

1. Start by curving from the headline down to the baseline.
2. Lift your pencil and start a new stroke to the right by curving from the headline to the midline.
3. Make a loop below to the midline and curve down to the baseline.
4. Finish with an undercurve.

Koala

Trace the letter and write it several times on each line.

Write the word "King."

Write the word "Jesus Christ is the King of Kings."

Provide extra practice as needed on separate lined paper.

Instructions

1. Start at the midline and curve up to the headline.
2. Loop back and down to the baseline.
3. Make a horizontal loop above the baseline.
4. Finish by curving below the baseline and back up to the baseline.

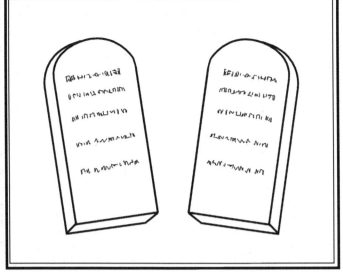

Law

Trace the letter and write it several times on each line.

L

L

L

L

Write the word "Lord."

Lord

Write the sentence "Love comes from God."

Provide extra practice as needed on separate lined paper.

$\mathcal{M} \; m \; m \; m$

Instructions

1. Start by curving at the headline down to the baseline.
2. Make an overcurve that goes halfway between the midline and the headline.
3. Make another overcurve that is a bit smaller.
4. Finish with an undercurve.

Mercy

Trace the letter and write it several times on each line.

m

m

m

m

Write the word "Michael."

Write the sentence "Micah was a prophet."

Provide extra practice as needed on separate lined paper.

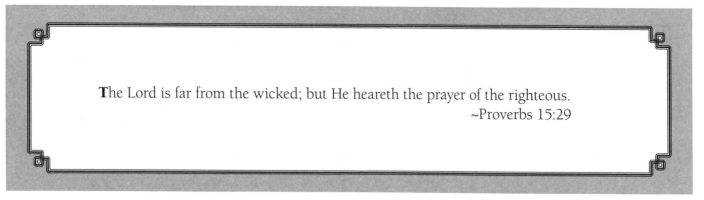

The Lord is far from the wicked; but He heareth the prayer of the righteous.

~Proverbs 15:29

Instructor Tips

We use our signatures to express who we are. Help your students develop a signature that they can call their own.

Chapter Check-up

Are you ready to write? Do your best work as you write out the following sentences.
All people are sinners. Jesus is the Lord of heaven and earth.

Answer the following questions.   Circle

1. Do all my letters slant in the same direction?   Yes   No
2. Am I shaping every letter correctly?   Yes   No
3. Are all the letters in one word connected?   Yes   No
4. Am I spacing letters evenly?   Yes   No
5. Am I leaving space between words?   Yes   No
6. Am I leaving extra space between sentences?   Yes   No
7. Am I remembering punctuation?   Yes   No
8. Am I remembering to capitalize?   Yes   No

Letters I write well:

Letters I need to practice:

n n n

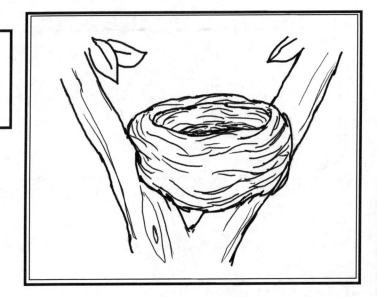

Instructions

1. Start by curving at the headline down to the baseline.
2. Make an overcurve that goes halfway between the midline and headline.
3. Finish with an undercurve.

Nest

Trace the letter and write it several times on each line.

n

n

n

n

Write the word "Noah."

Noah

Write the sentence "Noah built the ark."

Provide extra practice as needed on separate lined paper.

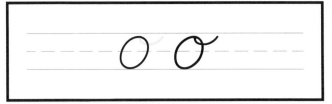

Instructions

1. Start by making a circle between the baseline and the headline. Make sure the circle touches the baseline.
2. Loop back to the right.

Owl

Trace the letter and write it several times on each line.

Write the word "Old."

Write the sentence "Our faith is in the Lord."

Provide extra practice as needed on separate lined paper.

Instructions

1. Start at the midline and curve up to the headline.
2. Make a straight line to the baseline.
3. Curve up to the headline.
4. Finish by looping back to where your second stroke crosses the midline.

Pray

Trace the letter and write it several times on each line.

P

P

P

P

Write the word "Peter."

Peter

Write the sentence "Peter prayed every day."

Provide extra practice as needed on separate lined paper.

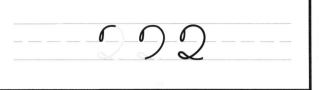

Instructions

1. Start a bit above the midline and loop up to the headline.
2. Continue to curve down to the baseline.
3. Finish by looping over to the right crossing your second stroke above the baseline.

Queen

Trace the letter and write it several times on each line.

Q

Q

Q

Q

Write the word "Quick."

Quick

Write the sentence "Queen Esther loved the Lord."

Provide extra practice as needed on separate lined paper.

Instructions

1. Start at the midline and curve up to the headline.
2. Make a straight line to the baseline.
3. Curve up to the headline and loop back to where your second stroke crosses the midline.
4. Loop up to the midline and curve down to the baseline.
5. Finish with an undercurve.

Radio

Trace the letter and write it several times on each line.

R

R

R

R

Write the word "Randy."

Randy

Write the sentence "Ruth was a faithful woman."

Provide extra practice as needed on separate lined paper.

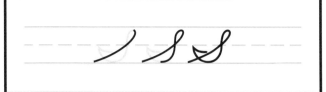

Instructions

1. Start at the baseline and curve up to the headline.
2. Loop back and make a double curve down to the baseline again.
3. Curve up to the midline and finish with a hook to the right.

Sabbath

Trace the letter and write it several times on each line.

Write the word "Savior."

Savior

Write the sentence "Sunday is the Christian Sabbath."

Provide extra practice as needed on separate lined paper.

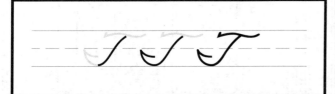

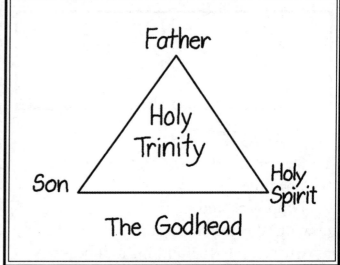

Instructions

1. Start a little under the headline and curve down to the baseline.
2. Continue the curve up to the midline and hook to the right.
3. Lift your pencil and, at the headline, make a notch and cross the "T" by making a horizontal double curve.

Trinity

Trace the letter and write it several times on each line.

Write the word "Timothy."

Timothy

Write the sentence "The Lord is one God in three persons."

Provide extra practice as needed on separate lined paper.

$\mathcal{U} \; \mathcal{V} \; \mathcal{U}$

Instructions

1. Start by curving at the headline down to the baseline.
2. Curve back up to the headline.
3. Curve down to the baseline again and finish with an undercurve.

Uncle

Trace the letter and write it several times on each line.

$\mathcal{U}$

$\mathcal{U}$

$\mathcal{U}$

$\mathcal{U}$

Write the word "United States."

United States

Write the sentence "Uncle Jim loves the Lord."

Provide extra practice as needed on separate lined paper.

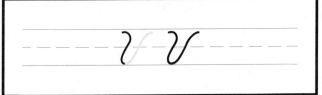

Instructions

1. Start by curving at the headline down to the baseline.
2. Finish by curving back up to the headline.

Vulture

Trace the letter and write it several times on each line.

Write the word "Vicky."

Write the sentence "My sister Vicky loves to worship."

Provide extra practice as needed on separate lined paper.

𝒰 𝒰 𝒰 𝒰

Instructions

1. Start by curving at the headline down to the baseline.
2. Curve back up to the headline.
3. Curve back down to the baseline.
4. Finish by curving back up to the headline.

Whale

Trace the letter and write it several times on each line.

𝒰

𝒰

𝒰

𝒰

Write the word "William."

William

Write the sentence "King William ruled well."

Provide extra practice as needed on separate lined paper.

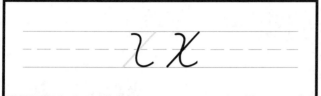

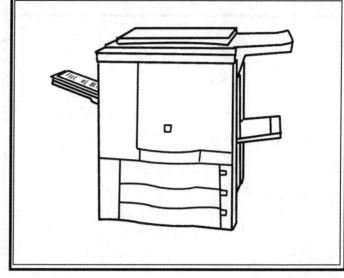

Instructions

1. Start at the headline and make a double curve down to the baseline.
2. Lift your pencil and cross the "X" from the head line to the baseline.

Xerox

Trace the letter and write it several times on each line.

X

X

X

X

Write the word "X-Ray."

X-ray

Write the sentence "The Xerox machine is broken."

Provide extra practice as needed on separate lined paper.

𝒴 𝒴 𝒴 𝒴

Instructions

1. Start by curving at the headline down to the baseline.
2. Curve back up to the headline.
3. Curve down below the baseline.
4. Loop up to just above the baseline crossing your third stroke at the baseline.

Yak

Trace the letter and write it several times on each line.

𝒴

𝒴

𝒴

𝒴

Write the word "Yosemite."

Yosemite

Write the sentence "You need to keep God's Law."

Provide extra practice as needed on separate lined paper.

Instructions

1. Start by curving at the headline down to the baseline.
2. Loop up and curve down below the baseline.
3. Loop back up just above the baseline crossing your second stroke at the baseline.

Zulu

Trace the letter and write it several times on each line.

Write the word "Zacharias."

Zacharias

Write the sentence "Zebras love to run."

Provide extra practice as needed on separate lined paper.

Practice: Days of the Week

Practice writing each day of the week six times in the space below. Instructors may wish to have their students make up a calendar on separate paper.

Sunday Monday Tuesday Wednesday Thursday Friday Saturday

Sunday

Monday

Tuesday

Wednesday

Thursday

Friday

Saturday

Practice: Months of the Year

Write out each of the months three times in the space below.

**January   February   March   April   May   June   July   August   September
October   November   December**

January February March
April May June July
August September October
November December

Writing Sentences in Cursive

Copy the sentences below in the space provided. Don't forget to include capital letters and punctuation.

In the beginning God created the heaven and the earth.

I will love thee, O Lord, my strength.

Every word of God is pure: he is a shield unto them that put their trust in him.

Writing Sentences in Cursive

Copy the sentences below in the space provided. Don't forget to include capital letters and punctuation.

Humble yourselves in the sight of the Lord, and he shall lift you up.

But thanks be to God, who giveth us the victory through our Lord Jesus Christ.

Thou shalt love thy neighbor as thyself.

Writing a Letter to a Friend

It is time for you to trace a short letter. Trace the copy of the letter that is written below. Study the way that this letter was written. See where the date, salutation, complimentary close, and signature are placed.

May 11, 2003

Date

Dear Grace,

Salutation

Please come to church

Body

services with me on

Sunday, May 19. Sunday

school begins at 9 a.m. We

will sing and rejoice as we

praise the Lord together at

Trinity Chapel. If you can

come, please let me know.

Your friend,

Complimentary Close

Beth

Signature

Writing a Letter to a Friend

Write your own letter, inviting a friend to your birthday party. Write out your letter on separate paper until it is in good order, then write your final version in the space below. Practice on a chalkboard or extra paper, as needed.

Date

Salutation

Body

Complimentary Close

Signature

Practice: The Ten Commandments

Copy each of the Ten Commandments written in cursive.

Thou shalt have no other gods before me.

Thou shalt not make unto thee any graven image.

Thou shalt not take the name of the Lord thy God in vain.

Remember the Sabbath day,
to keep it holy.

Honor thy father and thy
mother.

Thou shalt not murder.

Thou shalt not commit
adultery.

Thou shalt not steal.

*Thou shalt not bear
false witness against thy
neighbor.*

*Thou shalt not covet
anything that is thy
neighbor's.*

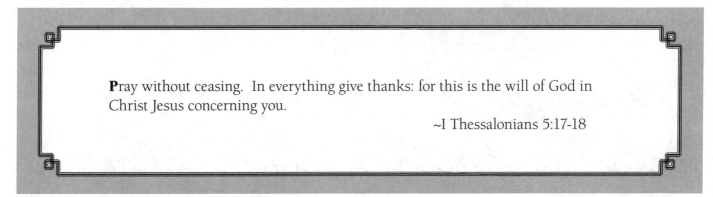

Pray without ceasing. In everything give thanks: for this is the will of God in Christ Jesus concerning you.

~I Thessalonians 5:17-18

Instructor Tips

Encourage your students to write their own thank-you cards and birthday invitations. Have them make a calendar for the current month.

Chapter Check-up

Are you ready to write? Do your best work as you copy these sentences.

The United States of America is large.
Our God rules over heaven and earth.

Answer the following questions.   Circle

1.	Do all my letters slant in the same direction?	Yes	No
2.	Am I shaping every letter correctly?	Yes	No
3.	Are all the letters in one word connected?	Yes	No
4.	Am I spacing letters evenly?	Yes	No
5.	Am I leaving extra space between words?	Yes	No
6.	Am I leaving extra space between sentences?	Yes	No
7.	Am I remembering punctuation?	Yes	No
8.	Am I remembering to capitalize?	Yes	No

Letters I write well:

Letters I need to practice:

Handwriting Teaching Suggestions

Seating arrangements are important for any instruction in handwriting. The instructor should make the best use of lighting so that the incidence of shadows on the student's papers will be minimized. Overhead lighting, which fill in most shadows and provides even illumination in all parts of the room, is best. Natural lighting should come at an angle so that the student's writing hand will not cast shadows on his paper. If the instructor is teaching handwriting to both left and right-handed students, they must be seated so that they do not interfere with one another.

Good posture affects handwriting. The student should sit comfortably in his chair with his feet on the floor. The desk should be slightly higher than the student's waist. The student should sit, not leaning to the left or to the right, but bending forward slightly. His forearms should rest on his desk.

The position of the paper is related to the student's posture. The student should place his paper in front of his eyes and under his writing hand. The non-writing hand lies on the paper to hold it still. The slant of the paper will allow him to see around his hand as he works. Thus, he will not have to lean to the left or the right to see his work. A right-handed student will tilt his paper to the right, 30-45 degrees. These paper positions will eliminate the hooked-hand position which restricts hand and finger movement needed for writing. The hooked-hand position must also be avoided to prevent poor posture.

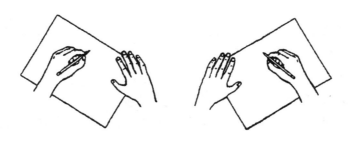

Handwriting Teaching Suggestions

The most desirable writing tool even for the beginning writer is a standard 2B pencil. This pencil is better suited to small hands than the extra-large pencil commonly thought to be good for small children. The pencil should be soft enough to mark readily and long enough to extend past the first knuckle of the hand.

The student's thumb and index finger should grasp the pencil, letting it rest on the middle finger. The last two fingers arch under the middle finger to support it. The hand rests on its side. The student should hold the pencil about one inch from the writing point. The pencil will point toward the shoulder. A student should hold his pencil lightly enough so it can be pulled from his hand with little resistance. In general, low or medium pressure produces better writing. Teaching correct pencil hold is one of the greatest responsibilities of the instructor. It is very difficult and often impossible to correct an improper hold that has become an established habit.

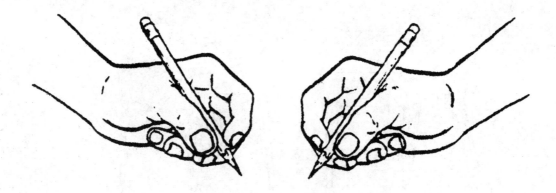

Writing at a chalkboard, if available, will help the student practice letter formations under the watchful eye of the instructor. The activity also allows for the development of the large muscles which are used in the writing process. If a chalkboard is not available, the student should be able to adequately complete most chalkboard exercises on a whiteboard or a hand-held slate.

The following guidelines should be followed to make chalkboard writing a meaningful activity:

1.   The student should stand comfortably about an arm's length from the chalkboard, allowing room for the elbow to bend at the proper angle (down and away from the body). Both feet should be on the floor.
2.   All writing should be done at the student's eye level.
3.   The chalk should be held between the thumb and the first two fingers. It should be long enough to be easily held.
4.   The writing should be done with light, sweeping strokes, with the end of the chalk rounded so that it will not squeak.

Handwriting Teaching Suggestions

Illegible handwriting is often a clue to the instructor that the student may have special learning problems. Some children cannot write well because they are not mature enough to acquire the motor skills which are necessary to form letters and words. Other children may have poor vision, a problem that a visit to an ophthalmologist will often solve. A small number of children have a specific learning disability which makes it difficult for them to remember the vast amount of information they are exposed to each day. Students with these major learning problems should be referred to a learning specialist for diagnosis and evaluation.

Uneven or illegible writing is often the result of letters that do not rest on the baseline. Improper letter height can produce an uneven top alignment. Even spacing between letters and words is also essential to legible writing.

The student can easily master letter formations if he follows the procedure listed below:

1. The instructor should verbalize the letter formation as the student writes each new letter. If the student has access to a chalkboard, he should use a different color of chalk for each stroke if a letter has more than one stroke.
2. The student should stand and air-trace the letter as the instructor verbalizes the letter formation again.
3. If a chalkboard is available, the student should once again write the letter on the board.
4. The student should begin practicing writing the letter on the writing pad. The instructor should periodically review the student's work to ensure that the student is following instructions.
5. When the student has adequately practiced writing the letter, he should complete the exercise in the workbook.

Neatness also contributes to legibility. The instructor should teach the student to eliminate undesirable handwriting by drawing one line through it rather than scribbling over or erasing it. Sometimes vigorous erasing eliminates both the writing and the paper. Of course, learning to erase small mistakes properly comes from instruction in handwriting also. The student must be taught to think about what he is writing to avoid careless errors, but the instructor must be realistic about the degree of neatness expected of the student.

Rhythm is the regularity of the pressure patterns of fingers on the writing instrument. When we write, we tend to put more pressure on the instrument as we draw the line down toward us and less pressure as we push it up and away. Because of the simple one-stroke letters, the student will begin to learn rhythm from the outset of instruction in handwriting. It will

Handwriting Teaching Suggestions

become a part of the student's writing when he begins to see whole words, when he attains a speed that is appropriate for his skill, and when he eliminates unnecessary tension from his pencil hold and small muscle movements. The student needs to attain consistency of rhythm before he works to increase his speed.

In order to be effective, the evaluation of handwriting should directly involve the student. A checklist should be displayed which the student can use to correct errors in his handwriting. This list should include the following questions:

1. Do I hold my pencil correctly?
2. Do I have good posture?
3. Are all my letters resting on the baseline?
4. Do all small letters touch the midline, and do all tall letters touch the top line?
5. Are the spaces between the letters and words even?
6. Do all my letters slant the same way?
7. Are all my downstrokes parallel?
8. Are all my letters with loops well formed?
9. Are all closed letters formed correctly?

By comparing past and present work, the student can be encouraged to improve his handwriting. The work can be kept in a writing folder and individual assignments for writing practice can be made from the papers. If this comparison is made on a regular basis, it will keep the student's attention centered on improvement and will help to positively motivate him.

Practice